ALL THE WOMEN I AM

Published on the occasion of the exhibition
Reba: All the Women I Am

Country Music Hall of Fame® and Museum
Opening August 2013

Written by Michael McCall
Foreword by Reba McEntire

COUNTRY MUSIC FOUNDATION PRESS
Nashville, Tennessee
2013

COUNTRY MUSIC FOUNDATION PRESS
222 Fifth Avenue South • Nashville, Tennessee 37203
(615) 416-2001

Copyright© 2013 by the Country Music Foundation, Inc. All rights reserved.
No part of this publication may be reproduced, stored in a retrieval system, or transmitted, in any form or by any means, electronic, mechanical, photocopying, recording, or otherwise without the prior written permission of the Country Music Foundation Press. Published 2013. Printed in the United States of America.
978-0-915608-20-1
This publication was created by the Staff of the Country Music Hall of Fame® and Museum.
Editors: Michael McCall and Jay Orr
Printer: Lithographics, Inc., Nashville, TN

Except in the Fashion and Friendship section, pages 48-57, all artifacts in this book
appear courtesy of Reba / Starstruck Entertainment.
Artifacts in that section appear courtesy of Reba / Starstruck Entertainment
and courtesy of Sandi Spika Borchetta.

CONTENTS

Introduction 4
Letter from the Director 6
Foreword 7

EARLY LIFE 8
The McEntire Way 10
The Young Cowgirl 12
A Competitive Spirit 14
Family Band 16

REBA BECOMES A STAR 18
Mercury Years 20
Her Kind of Country 22
Whoever's in New England 26
The Rising Superstar 30
Starstruck Entertainment 32

MULTI-PLATINUM DECADE 34
New Frontiers 36
Tragedy in the Air 38
A Broken-Hearted Return 40
Creative Partnerships 44
Fashion and Friendship 48
Life on Top 58

ACTING 62
Drama Queen 64
Expanding Her Roles 66
On Broadway 70
Reba Triumphs on TV 74
South Pacific 78
A Return to Comedy 80

AMERICAN ICON 82
A Musical Journal 84
Still Climbing Mountains 86
The Reba Brand 88
An Entertaining Host 90
Two Close Friends,
Two Strong Voices 94
Connecting to a Big Machine 96
Top of the Mountain 98

Acknowledgments 102

INTRODUCTION

In 1976, Reba McEntire made her Nashville recording debut with "I Don't Want to Be a One Night Stand." She need not have worried. As we now know, Reba would go on to rank among the most enduring and widely recognized entertainers of her—or any—generation.

From the start, Reba's artistic gifts were breathtaking. Before she ever arrived in Nashville, she drew notice for a big voice that could soar with the power and expressiveness of the best singers in any genre.

However, achieving career longevity requires more than talent; it requires hard work, perseverance, a willingness to gamble, and an ability to evolve, change, and stay abreast of trends. No one has proven more determined to put in the work, or to throw the dice, than the small-town Okie redhead we all have come to know on a first-name-only basis, Reba.

The Country Music Hall of Fame and Museum chose to call its exhibition *Reba: All the Women I Am* not only because it was the title of the singer's 2011 album, but because it aptly describes her multitude of talents and how she has grown from a spunky, girl-next-door cowgirl to a glamorous queen of stage and screen.

Moreover, the exhibition title underscores one of Reba's primary talents: that is, to become wholly invested in all the different characters she has portrayed in lyrics and in scripts. What a treat it must be for those who write songs and scripts to hear Reba bring their creations to life and fill them with such believable emotions.

Like the best artists, Reba stepped up to represent perfectly the changes going on in American society at the time of her success. Most of the country queens who influenced Reba—Kitty Wells, Patsy Cline, Loretta Lynn, Dottie West, Tammy Wynette—sang about struggles at home, about society's expectations of them, and about the men in their lives. Reba surfaced just as the women's liberation movement reached the suburbs and the Southland, and women began competing with male counterparts in business and beyond.

Reba's early songs dealt primarily with relationships, as in the mid-1980s when she scored the #1 hits "How Blue," "Somebody Should Leave," and "Whoever's in New England." But as her 1992 #1 hit "Is There Life Out There" suggested, a world of experiences existed beyond the kitchen and the bedroom for women. More women were starting businesses, rising to executive positions, confronting problems with sexism, and speaking out with force and, at times, with charm about the societal changes they wanted to push forward. Reba's work began representing the broader dreams and goals of other women, and she started singing about social issues and about what it took for an ambitious woman to survive and to climb new mountains—all while adapting a sassy, outspoken tone toward anyone who would dare hold her back or do her wrong.

Like Rosanne Cash and Emmylou Harris in the 1980s, and Faith Hill and Martina McBride in the 1990s, Reba represented the way women had evolved and changed with the times. She barreled through old barriers with a down-home attitude that appealed to older and younger fans alike in ways that her more urban and rock-influenced peers did not. Reba followed the lead of her hero Dolly Parton in tackling fields far beyond country music. Like Dolly, she succeeded in erasing boundaries, and she achieved a broad-based success rare for country singers of any gender and generation.

When Reba won the CMA Entertainer of the Year award in 1986—becoming only the fourth woman to do so—she recalled arriving in Nashville and being warned that, as a woman and a country singer, she shouldn't set her sights too high in the entertainment business. "Y'all just proved them wrong," Reba said.

Since then, Reba has continued to prove them wrong, over and over again, and in ways even she could not have foreseen. This book traces her triumphant story, through setback and tragedy and joyous conquest. As this book reveals, Reba is always looking forward; the Country Music Hall of Fame and Museum appreciates the opportunity she has provided to look back at all she has accomplished—so far.

—**Michael McCall**

August 2013

Dear Museum Friend,

Raised on an Oklahoma ranch, Reba Nell McEntire was hoisted onto a western saddle at a very young age. While other kids were riding stick horses and playing with cap pistols, Reba became an accomplished real-life cowhand. Blessed with a limber alto, remarkable moxie, and a genius work ethic, Reba soon rose from barrel-racing rodeo tomboy to country music star *par excellence*.

Like Jean Shepard and Loretta Lynn before her, Reba recorded music that spoke to new generations of women and inspired countless numbers to have the courage to change their lives. Like Aretha, Cher, and Dolly, she became a one-name show queen who starred on Broadway, in her own television sitcom, and in various titles on the big screen. She became a prosperous entrepreneur and now reigns as the most successful female country performer of her generation. In 2011, reflecting her many notable contributions to the growth and popularity of America's music, Reba was inducted into the Country Music Hall of Fame.

In keeping with our educational mission, we have been archiving Reba's music and story since her 1976 debut on Mercury/Polygram, continuing through her decades on MCA and her current partnership with Scott Borchetta's Valory Music Company. Her generous donations of career memorabilia and loans of other key artifacts have often been included in our core exhibit, *Sing Me Back Home: A Journey through Country Music*.

In 2002, we introduced a spotlight exhibit featuring many costumes worn by Reba in her starring role as Annie Oakley in the 2001 Broadway production of *Annie Get Your Gun*. In 2009, we showcased the eye-popping red dress with the plunging neckline that shocked some when the superstar wore it for her performance of "Does He Love You" with Linda Davis on the 1993 CMA Awards telecast. Following her induction into the Country Music Hall of Fame, she was featured in an annual museum exhibit devoted to the current honorees.

Reba's guest appearances on our stage have included performances at three Medallion Ceremonies including the Country Music Hall of Fame inductions of Harold Bradley (2006), the Statler Brothers (2008), and Barbara Mandrell (2009).

It is our great honor to be entrusted with the stewardship of Reba's music and story. This exhibit, *Reba: All the Women I Am*, will remain open until June 2014. The exhibit story will be accompanied by related live performances, panels, films, and other programs enhanced by records, film and video clips, and other properties from our collection. Some of these will be streamed live at www.countrymusichalloffame.org, where you can also find a schedule of all Museum programs.

Sincerely,

Kyle Young, Director
Country Music Hall of Fame® and Museum

FOREWORD

I have been many women throughout my career of thirty-seven years (and counting). In my songs, I have been a storyteller; an angry, left behind woman; an optimist; a best friend; a mother; an encourager; a forever dreamer; a survivor; the last one to know; and a prostitute gone good. I have enjoyed being each and every character in the songs I sing, and I thank the songwriters for creating such vivid characters for me.

I'm a pack rat at heart, and I'm so happy that I kept clothes and other souvenirs from my growing-up years and my stage shows, movies, videos, and TV series. I even have the program from the first time I sang into a microphone. It was the first grade, and I was in the Kiowa grade-school Christmas show. I'm even happier that the Country Music Hall of Fame® and Museum has asked to put some of my items in an exhibit and in this companion book. I was running out of room!

I kept these personal objects because I enjoy looking back and remembering. These items jog my memory. I look at a dress, and I go back to being on stage and looking out at an audience. I see a pantsuit, and I remember the kitchen on the *Reba* TV show where I wore it. Great memories from wonderful things I have had the privilege to do in my life. I thank the Lord daily for my memories.

I hope you enjoy this walk down memory lane with me. Please know that there is love in every object you see. Love and memories: two things very dear to me.

Love,

Reba

Left to right: Reba, Pendleton Round-Up Rodeo Queen, Jacqueline McEntire, Clark McEntire, and Pake McEntire gathered around the saddle awarded to Clark on the night he became the 1957 champion steer roper at the Pendleton Round-Up rodeo in Oregon.

Early Life

Right: Susie, Pake, Reba, and Alice McEntire, 1958.

Middle right: Reba's third-grade photo.

Far right: Reba, July 1956.

Below: Jacqueline and Clark McEntire with their children (left to right): Susie, Pake, Reba, and Alice.

The McEntire Way

Working hard, setting ambitious goals, striving to be the best: these traits came naturally to Reba McEntire, because they were instilled in her as she grew up.

The Country Music Hall of Fame member was born Reba Nell McEntire on March 28, 1955, in McAlester, Oklahoma, the daughter of rodeo champion Clark McEntire and schoolteacher and homemaker Jacqueline Smith McEntire.

Clark and Jackie owned an eight-thousand-acre ranch in Chockie, Oklahoma. He arose before sunrise each morning, rustled up his four children and put them to work on the ranch. Reba was six years old when she began helping manage more than three thousand head of cattle. Along with sisters Alice and Susie and brother Pake, she rode horses to round up livestock and took on responsibilities such as branding, castrating, vaccinating, and de-worming—work she continued to do through her high school years.

> For the Clark McEntires it's a girl, born March 28th. The little miss has been named Reba. This makes two girls and a boy for Clark and Jackie who live near Kiowa, Okla.

Announcement in the May 1955 issue of *Hoofs and Horns* magazine.

The Young Cowgirl

Pake and Reba McEntire, 1958.

For the McEntires and other families in the hills of Oklahoma, working the ranch was a harsh yet necessary reality, day in and day out. Eventually, for Reba, applying herself *off* the ranch became a means for escape and for enriching a life otherwise dominated by hard work.

Reba used the skills she learned on the ranch—especially mounting her horse to round up cattle—to compete on the rodeo circuit. She followed in the boot prints of her grandfather John McEntire, 1934 world champion steer roper, and her father, a three-time world-champion steer roper. Rodeo events were a regular part of Reba's upbringing. She started competing in rodeo barrel racing at age eleven. Before her music career took off, she participated in more than fifty rodeos a year.

Clark McEntire and the J.J. Hanley Trophy saddle awarded to him at the 1957 Pendleton Round-Up, where he won the steer roping championship.
Saddle photo by Bob Delevante.

Reba in a 1975 barrel racing competition at Fort Smith, Arkansas.

Reba with her horse, Sonny, at the family ranch, 1978.

A Competitive Spirit

When Reba was in second grade, her mother Jackie accepted a job at the Kiowa School District to organize the library. She stayed on to become secretary for superintendent Harold Toaz. She also encouraged her kids to become involved in school activities.

Reba followed her mother's advice and became active in sports and music. "My energy and aggression found a healthy outlet in fifth grade athletics," the singer wrote in her autobiography, *Reba: My Story*.

Above: Reba (standing, far left) with her high school basketball team, the Kiowa Cowgirls.

Right: I.D. badge for the 1972 Oklahoma high school basketball championship.

Far right: Reba at a basketball camp in Eufala, Oklahoma.

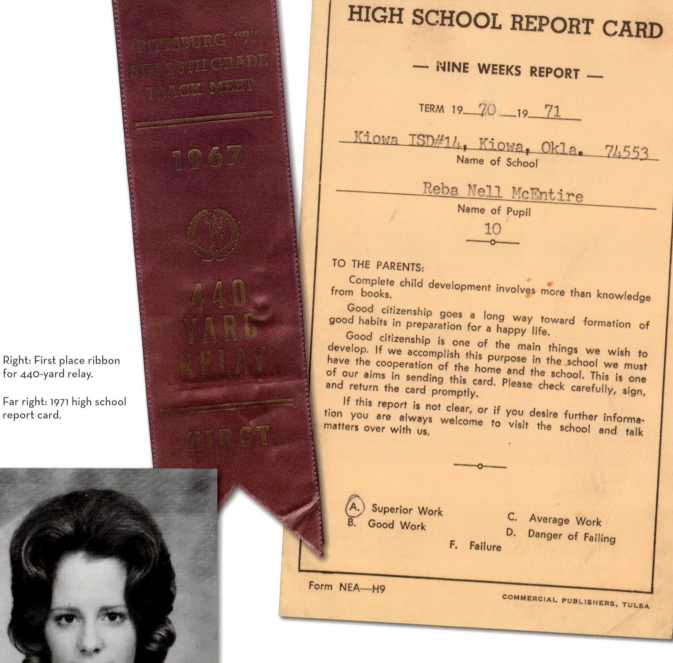

Right: First place ribbon for 440-yard relay.

Far right: 1971 high school report card.

Senior-class photo at Kiowa High.

A sprinter in track, Reba set a fifth-grade record for the seventy-five-yard dash that stood for decades. She also started at guard on the basketball team, from the fifth grade through her senior year, when she helped Kiowa High reach the Oklahoma state championship final.

Reba's desire to perform and her competitive nature, already evident, would become constants in her life.

The Singing McEntires—Susie, Reba, and Pake—reunited for a *Nashville Now* performance on TNN.

Top left: First time behind a microphone, singing "Away in a Manger" at the Kiowa Christmas program in first grade.

Top right: The Kiowa High School Cowboy Band, with (from left) Pake McEntire, Gary Raiborn, Susie McEntire, Kelly Rhyne, Reba, and Roger Wills.

Above: 1975 concert poster.

Family Band

Reba grew up with music. Her mother, Jackie, loved to sing, as did her brother, Pake, and her sister Susie. Except for oldest sister Alice—who had a beautiful voice but chose to concentrate on rodeo instead—all of the McEntire siblings gained recognition for their singing talents.

Of Reba's extracurricular activities, music was the most important. She won her first talent contest in fifth grade, at a 4-H club competition, singing "My Sweet Little Alice Blue Gown." Later, she joined with Pake, Susie, and other musical classmates in the Kiowa High School Cowboy Band, which was started by Reba's mother and history and art instructor Clark Rhyne. One band member, bassist Roger Wills, went on to become a highly regarded Nashville musician and a longtime member of Alan Jackson's band.

Later, Reba, Pake, and Susie formed the Singing McEntires, which became a popular regional group with a busy concert schedule. All three began to consider grander possibilities beyond the Oklahoma border. Eventually they each signed recording contracts and pursued musical careers—but it was Reba who took the first big step.

Singing the national anthem at the 1976 National Finals Rodeo in Oklahoma City.

Reba Becomes a Star

Mercury Years

In December 1974, country singer Red Steagall heard Reba perform the national anthem in Oklahoma City at the National Finals Rodeo competition, and later the same week he listened as she sang a cappella at a hotel party for rodeo industry guests. Impressed, Steagall paid for a Nashville recording session with Reba and played the tape for Music Row record executives.

Glenn Keener of Polygram/Mercury Records loved Reba's voice and signed her to the record label in November 1975. She struggled at first: her first ten singles, heavy on ballads, failed to reach the *Billboard* country singles Top Ten. Even after her first #1 hit, in 1983, she continued to have only sporadic success. Most of the recordings featured highly polished, middle-of-the-road, pop-influenced productions—the prevalent country sound of the time.

Reba knew she needed a change to save her career. Her last single for Mercury was prophetic: "There Ain't No Future in This."

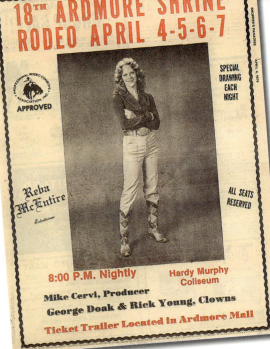

Above: Jukebox title strip for "You're the First Time I've Thought About Leaving," Reba's second #1 hit, in 1983.

Top left: Reba with Red Steagall.

Left: Ardmore, Oklahoma, rodeo poster, 1979.

Right: Stage outfit from the 1970s, made by Millie Wilson, the wife of Reba's school bus driver. *Photo by Bob Delevante.*

Far Right: Autographing her 1977 self-titled first album, Fan Fair 1978.

Below: Reba's first single, released in 1976.

Accepting the 1984 CMA Female Vocalist of the Year award.

Her Kind of Country

Above: 1986 CMA Female Vocalist of the Year envelope.

Right: 1986 CMA Entertainer of the Year Award.
Photo by Bob Delevante.

Reba signed with MCA in 1984, hoping a different record company could help her fledgling career. But only one song from her first MCA album reached the Top Ten, which didn't alter her b-level status.

By now, Reba had spent nearly a decade in the music industry, and she had begun to trust her own instincts. She decided she would stand out more if she went against the prevalent trends of the time, so she persuaded MCA label chief Jimmy Bowen to let her create an album of traditional country music. Her wish was to exchange the orchestra for a steel guitar and fiddle. Bowen said yes. Two new songs became #1 hits: "How Blue" and "Somebody Should Leave."

Reba finally had achieved the momentum that previously had eluded her. In the fall of 1984, she won her first CMA Award, for Female Vocalist of the Year. She went on to become the first woman ever to win CMA Female Vocalist of the Year honors in four consecutive years.

In 1986, she won the prestigious CMA Entertainer of the Year award, a rare achievement for a woman in country music at the time. After years of struggle, Reba had jumped to the top of the country music field—but only after she started making her own career decisions. It was a lesson she never forgot.

Right: The cover of the 1984 album *My Kind of Country*.

Below: Engraved silver and gold commemorative belt buckle, with a pair of inset diamonds, presented to Reba in 1987 by the Smith Brothers for singing the national anthem at more than ten National Finals Rodeo events.
Photo by Bob Delevante.

Right: George Jones congratulated Reba for being named the 1985 CMA Female Vocalist of the Year.

```
                                    1985 OCT 16 PM 1:23

     NAS
FOMASTER    1-012342C289 10/16/85
PMPTUL PTL
05261 10-16 1110A PDT PTUI
786553 WU AGT NAS

REPORT DELIVERY BY MAILGRAM/
4-0197745289 10/16/85
ICS IPMBNGZ CSP
  4098375463 TDBN COLMESNEIL TX 78 10-16 0114P EST
PMS REBA MCENTIRE,   SPENCE MANOR RPT DLY MGM, DLR
116 MUSIC SQUARE E
NASHVILLE TN 37203

CONGRATULATIONS ON RECEIVING YOUR AWARD AS COUNTRY MUSIC'S FEMALE
VOCALIST OF THE YEAR. IT IS AN AWARD YOU SO RICHLY DESERVE. IT IS
LIKE A BREATH OF FRESH AIR TO SEE A TRADITIONAL COUNTRY ARTIST BEING
RECOGNIZED. THANK YOU FOR BEING COUNTRY AND KEEPING TRADITIONAL
COUNTRY MUSIC ALIVE. IT MAKES ME VERY HAPPY KNOWING THAT OUR BELOVED
COUNTRY MUSIC HAS HOPES OF SURVIVING WHEN TRADITIONAL COUNTRY ARTISTS
LIKE YOURSELF RECEIVE AWARDS THAT RECOGNIZE THEIR TALENT AND MUSIC.
SINCERELY
   GEORGE JONES
   HWY 255
   COLMESNEIL TX 75938
1315 EST

NNNN
   REPLACES CHAR(S) ON SENDERS KEYBD UNAVAIL ON YOURS
```

Above: Red Steagall letter, 1986.

Right: Suede gown, designed by Tim Cobb, and worn by Reba when she accepted the 1986 CMA Entertainer of the Year award. *Photo by Bob Delevante.*

Whoever's in New England

Her success with older country styles aligned Reba with the new traditionalist movement in country music, which found young stars such as Ricky Skaggs and George Strait recording songs that drew more on classic country arrangements than on pop-crossover productions. She would cut a second successful traditional album, *Have I Got a Deal for You*, featuring the Texas fiddle of Johnny Gimble and the steel guitar of Weldon Myrick.

Reba wasn't done taking risks. Her 1986 album, *Whoever's in New England*, shifted back toward a crossover sound, but in a manner that had more musical and emotional depth than her earlier pop-leaning collections. Co-produced by Reba with MCA Nashville chief Jimmy Bowen, *Whoever's in New England* showed a more elegant side of the singer's artistry. It became her first gold album and featured two #1 hits: the title ballad and the up-tempo "Little Rock."

Above: Winner's card, 1986 ACM Awards.

Next page (from left): Red Steagall, MCA Records executive Bruce Hinton, Reba, manager Bill Carter, *Nashville Now* TV host Ralph Emery.

Above: Signing for the album *What Am I Gonna Do About You*, c. 1986.

In 1987, Reba rolled the dice again, taking a headlining gig at New York's prestigious Carnegie Hall, which rarely featured contemporary country stars. The concert was a sold-out success, and Reba's bright-eyed, flame-haired, sophisticated cowgirl persona was embraced by New Yorkers and their hard-to-impress media.

In a matter of three years, at MCA, Reba had become a national star reaching beyond country's borders.

The cover of the album *What Am I Gonna Do About You*.

DAILY NEWS 35

EXTRA ENTERTAINMENT

Howdy, Carnegie Hall

By BILL BELL
Daily News Staff Writer

REBA McENTIRE'S voice is a million-dollar treat that curls, slurs, blurs, breaks, slips and dips with hurtin'-to-high-heaven emotion and cowgirl spunk. The most dominant and honored woman in country music, she is an irresistible bundle of grits and glitz.

So why is she nervous about her Carnegie Hall debut tonight? "New Yorkers are different," she says. "They're used to sophisticated entertainment."

That's open for discussion, but McEntire shouldn't worry. She has a style—part sass, part brass—that New Yorkers will find tough to resist.

A few weeks ago, McEntire, 33, won the Country Music Association's female vocalist award for a fourth consecutive year. Tammy Wynette and Loretta Lynn won three in a row, but nobody—male or female—had ever won four straight.

Her two latest albums, including her newest, "The Last One to Know" (MCA), are among the Top 10 best sellers on country lists. Interestingly, they also are on the Billboard best-selling *pop* charts. Not bad for someone who still needs two syllables to pronounce "lips," "him" and other lyric standbys.

Despite the drawl, an Oklahoma background and a wardrobe that mixes fancy frocks and metal belt buckles the size of Econoline hubcaps, McEntire is not a hillbilly singer. She's a chirpy, perky ballad singer—"a sort-of soprano"—who dabbles in ladylike boogie and Western swing and can break a teamster's heart.

Her songs, which are for and about women, are growing bolder. The one-time rodeo competitor, who once sang catchy traditional tunes with titles like "I Don't Need Nothin' You Ain't Got," is now singing about wife-beating and divorce.

The style is something Nashville calls "neo-traditional," meaning fairly uncomplex melodies, down-to-earth lyrics and not so many horns, strings and backup singers. "I don't sing country," says McEntire, who does. "I don't sing pop. I just sing Reba songs."

It took her a decade of ex- and fine-tuning

'I always knew what I wanted,' says Reba McEntire. 'The thing was, I wasn't sure which way to get there'

FEELING RESTLESS: Reba McEntire wants it all.

wanted," she says. "The thing was, I wasn't sure which way to get there."

At a New York party last year, which she combined with a shopping spree, McEntire said that she didn't think her hectic career and private life—as the wife of a rancher and rodeo competitor—would

stayed in Stringtown, Okla., and she moved to Nashville. The problem, she said, was her restlessness.

THE RESTLESSNESS COincided with McEntire's realization that she was on the verge of really taking off. "I used to say it'd make me happy to record a few hits," she said. "Not now, un-

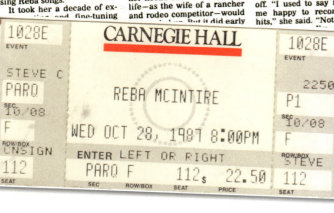

Ticket to Carnegie Hall concert.

Above: *New York Daily News* article on Reba's Carnegie Hall concert.

Right: On stage at Carnegie Hall, 1987.

From left: MCA Records executives Tony Brown and Al Teller, Reba, MCA's Bruce Hinton, and Narvel Blackstock, celebrating Reba's RIAA designation of platinum sales for her 1987 *Greatest Hits* album and gold for her 1989 *Sweet Sixteen* album.

The Rising Superstar

Reaching the top of the country music world only added fuel to Reba's ambitions. In the late 1980s, she remained as determined as ever to gain control of all aspects of her career, to ensure that it kept expanding and moving forward.

When first husband Charlie Battles suggested she slow down now that she had achieved so much, she realized he no longer understood the woman she had become. After her 1987 divorce, she relocated her home and business headquarters from Oklahoma to Nashville.

Reba also changed management, hiring her road manager and steel guitarist, Narvel Blackstock, to replace Bill Carter. In June 1989, Reba and Narvel married; they welcomed their son, Shelby, into their lives on February 23, 1990.

Meanwhile, Reba dominated the country charts, with nine #1s and three additional Top Ten hits from 1986 to 1989. Her concerts expanded into big-time extravaganzas, featuring state-of-the-art lights, video, costuming, and stage production—foreshadowing the rise of high-tech shows by Garth Brooks, Kenny Chesney, and others.

Top: With baby Shelby Blackstock, 1990.

Left: With Narvel Blackstock at their wedding, June 3, 1989.

Starstruck Entertainment

Lobby of Starstruck Entertainment, Nashville, Tennessee.

Starstruck Entertainment grew out of Reba's realization that no one understood her potential and goals as well as she did. Her recording career floundered until she took control of her musical direction. Wouldn't other aspects of her career benefit from a hands-on approach, too?

In 1988, she formed Starstruck Entertainment with manager (and soon-to-be husband) Narvel Blackstock. By the mid-1990s, Starstruck comprised artist management, promotion and concert booking, publicity, recording facilities, song publishing, transportation (including a charter air service), a construction company, and a horse farm. "In this business, the sky's the limit," Reba said in 1995.

In recent years, Reba has decided to simplify her life and her busy schedule. Starstruck now concentrates on artist management (Kelly Clarkson and Blake Shelton are clients), managing a state-of-the-art recording studio and broadcast studio, and working its publishing catalog.

Collectible lunchbox created in 2000 by Starstruck Entertainment.
Photo by Bob Delevante.

Boarding a Starstruck jet.

Multi-Platinum Decade

New Frontiers

Reba started the 1990s with a new husband, a new baby boy, a new record producer, and the same ambitious attitude.

When Tony Brown became president of MCA Nashville, he began producing Reba's records, taking over from former label head Jimmy Bowen, who had left to run a different company. Brown had a proven track record, having produced major hits for Rodney Crowell, Vince Gill, Patty Loveless, Steve Wariner, and others. He would become one of Reba's most trusted creative advisors, producing her records on and off between 1990 and 2009.

Brown and Reba first collaborated on *Rumor Has It*, one of her most successful albums, with more than three million in sales. The album's first single, "You Lie," was Reba's first #1 in more than a year. Another song from the album, a cover of Bobbie Gentry's "Fancy," stalled at #8 on the charts, but became an enduring fan favorite and a continuing show stopper for the flamboyant redhead.

Left: The cover of the album *Rumor Has It*, 1990.

Top left and far left: An elaborate stage dress that opened up to allow Reba to emerge, 1993.

MCA RECORDS
NASHVILLE
1701 WEST END AVE.
SUITE 400
NASHVILLE, TN 37203
615/244-8944

October 21, 1986

Ms. Reba McEntire
Star Route
Stringtown, OK 74569

Dear Reba,

To the prettiest "Entertainer Of The Year" ever. Congratulations on winning the awards the other night. I thought your speech was great, and it is wonderful to see recognition come to someone who deserves it so much. May it be the first of many "Entertainer Of The Year" awards.

Your Biggest Fan

Tony Brown

P.S. Your dress was awesome!

Record producer and MCA Records executive Tony Brown with a 1993 Harley-Davidson Heritage Softtail Classic, given to him by Reba that year.

Top: Letter to Reba from Tony Brown.

Right: Reba on stage, after emerging from the dress on the previous page.

Reba's road band, c. 1990. Kneeling, front: Joe McGlohon, saxophone.
Second row, left to right: Kirk Cappello, musical director, keyboards; Tony Saputo, drums.
Back row, left to right: Paula Kaye Evans, vocals; Michael Thomas, guitar; Joey Cigainero, synthesizer; Terry Jackson, bass; Suzy Wills, vocals.
Cappello, Saputo, Evans, Thomas, Cigainero, and Jackson were killed in the 1991 plane crash that also took the lives of musician Chris Austin (bottom right), road manager Jim Hammon (top right), and pilots Donald Holmes and Christopher Hollinger. *Band photo by Beth Gwinn*

Tragedy in the Air

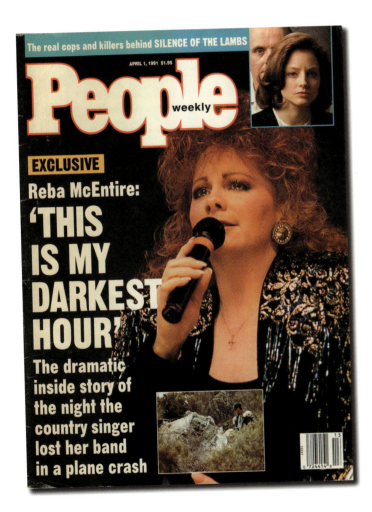

Cover of *People* magazine, April 1, 1991.

Reba, her band, and her crew interrupted a tour of the Midwest on March 15, 1991, to travel to San Diego for a concert. Private planes were chartered. On the return flight, one plane—a twin-engine Hawker Siddeley—clipped an outcropping of rock near the peak of Otay Mountain, causing the plane to crash. No one survived. The deceased were band members Chris Austin, Kirk Capello, Joey Cigainero, Paula Kaye Evans, Terry Jackson, Tony Saputo, and Michael Thomas; road manager Jim Hammon; and pilots Donald Holmes and Christopher Hollinger.

About that day, Reba wrote:

There are some dates in your life that you'll never forget. For me, it's March 16, 1991. We had played a private show in San Diego, and the band and part of the crew were flying in two private planes to Ft. Wayne, Indiana, for a show the following night.

One plane made it, the other is still on Otay Mountain outside of San Diego, just north of the Mexican border. Seven band members, my tour manager, and two pilots went to a better place that night. Two band members, the rest of the crew, and I were left to try and somehow go on with our lives.

Before San Diego, I had been looking for songs for the next album. I had to press on. When you're happy, you choose happy songs. When you're sad . . .

In the recording studio, bass player Leland Sklar looked at me and said, "Reba, are we ever gonna record a happy song?" I said, "Not on this album." For My Broken Heart *was the album title, and it reflects the mood of the twelve songs I recorded in 1991.*

Cover of Reba's 1991 album, *For My Broken Heart*.

A Broken-Hearted Return

Reba responded to the tragedy involving her band by releasing the subdued yet emotionally charged album *For My Broken Heart*. The album sold more than four million copies. The devastating sudden deaths of so many band members might have waylaid many artists. By pouring her emotions into her music, Reba created what is, so far, the best-selling studio album of her career.

Left: Satin-and-beaded gown, designed by Sandi Spika and worn by Reba at the 1992 ACM Awards.
Photo by Bob Delevante.

Liz Hengber's handwritten lyrics for the #1 hit, "For My Broken Heart," co-written by Hengber and Keith Palmer.

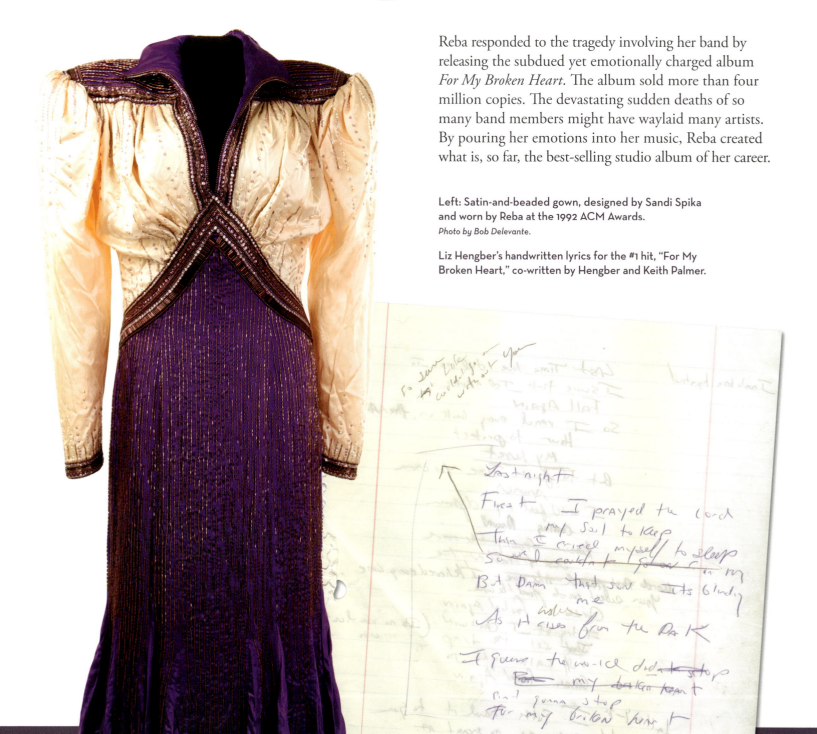

Holding her trophy for the ACM Top Female Vocalist award, 1991.

Right: Stage gown, designed by Sandi Spika, worn by Reba when performing "Fancy" on her 1992 tour. *Photo by Bob Delevante.*

The poignant title song reached #1, as did the next single, "Is There Life Out There." The latter became another of her many landmark career hits. "We started getting letters from people about how that song had changed their life or motivated them," Reba said in a *Los Angeles Times* interview in 1994, explaining why the hit song led to a CBS movie of the week. *Is There Life Out There?* starred Reba as a housewife and mother who enrolls in college.

Above: Reba with the actors who played her children in the TV film *Is There Life Out There?* (From left): Kyle Hudgens, Blair Struble, and Genia Michaela.

Top left: Reba in the TV film *Is There Life Out There?*

Left: With Huey Lewis on the set of the video for the song "Is There Life Out There."

Creative Partnerships

Reba's two albums at the start of the 1990s—*Rumor Has It* and *For My Broken Heart*—were starkly different from each other in musical tone and direction. But both achieved multi-platinum sales, setting the tone for her most successful decade as a recording artist. She went on to compile twenty-six Top Ten hits and to sell more than twenty million albums in North America in the 1990s.

Reba continued to experiment with new ideas. Only one true duet in her career had reached the charts—with Jacky Ward way back in 1978. But duets continually gave her a boost in the 1990s.

The hits started when "The Heart Won't Lie," a duet with Vince Gill, went to #1 in early 1993; "Does He Love You," a duet with Linda Davis, not only went to #1 in late 1993, it also won a Grammy for Best Country Vocal Collaboration and a CMA award for Vocal Event of the Year.

Top right: On the set of the TV sitcom *Evening Shade*. Standing: Burt Reynolds and Marilu Henner. Seated: Vince Gill and Reba.

Right: Vince Gill with Reba on the set of the video for the song "The Heart Won't Lie," 1993.

Grammy Award given to Reba and Linda Davis for 1993 Best Country Vocal Collaboration, for their chart-topping duet, "Does He Love You."

Top: Linda Davis with Reba backstage at the 1993 CMA Awards, where they performed "Does He Love You."

Right: Linda Davis and Reba McEntire on the set of the music video for "Does He Love You."

Near the end of the decade, Reba joined forces with Brooks & Dunn for the hit "If You See Him/If You See Her." The song reached #1 in 1998 and became a showcase number on a major concert tour featuring the two acts as co-headliners.

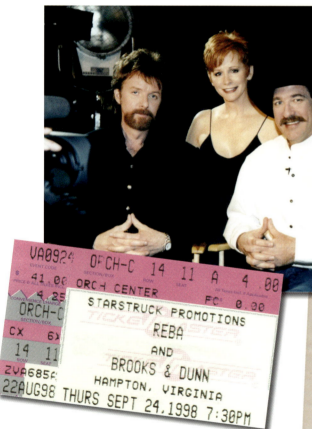

Ticket stub from a co-headlining concert featuring Reba and Brooks & Dunn.

Top: Promotional photograph with (from left) Ronnie Dunn and Kix Brooks.

Right: *Cash Box* country singles chart from 1978 with the song "Three Sheets in the Wind," a Reba duet with Jacky Ward, at #61.

CASH BOX TOP 100

May 20, 1978

#	Title	Artist	Weeks On 5/13	Chart
1	I'M ALWAYS ON A MOUNTAIN WHEN I FALL	MERLE HAGGARD (MCA 40869)	3	10
2	DO YOU KNOW YOU ARE MY SUNSHINE	THE STATLER BROTHERS (Mercury 55022)	5	10
3	GEORGIA ON MY MIND	WILLIE NELSON (Columbia 3-10704)	6	9
4	NO, NO, NO (I'D RATHER BE FREE)	Rex Allen, Jr. (Warner Bros. WBS-8541)	7	9
5	NIGHT TIME MAGIC	LARRY GATLIN (Monument 45-249)	9	6
6	WRONG, BUT IT'S ALL RIGHT	DOLLY PARTON (RCA PB-11240)	2	10
7	ON OVERTIME AT HOME	CHARLIE RICH (United Artists UA-X1193-Y)	10	7
8	SHE PUT HER SHOES	JOHNNY DUNCAN (Columbia 3-10694)	1	11
9	MY BED (ANYTIME)	EMMYLOU HARRIS (Warner Bros. WBS 8553)	17	6
10	FOUR BOTTLES OF WINE			
11	I CAN TOUCH HER AT ALL	WILLIE NELSON (RCA PB-11235)	12	10
12	LADIES DON'T GET LUCKY ALL THE TIME	GENE WATSON (Capitol P-4556)	16	6
13	I QUIT LOOKIN' AT YOU	DAVE & SUGAR (RCA PB-11251)	15	7
14	RED AND BLUE MEMORIES	JOE STAMPLEY (Epic 8-50517)	14	10
15	ME IN A JUG/ME AND THE	JOHNNY PAYCHECK (Epic 8-50539)	20	6
16	POWER OF POSITIVE	MICKEY GILLEY (Playboy ZS8-5826)	4	10
17	I'M GONNA LOVE YOU ANYWAY	TOM T. HALL (RCA PB-11253)	21	7
18	I CAN'T WAIT ANY LONGER	CRISTY LANE (LS/GRT-156)	18	9
19	THIS IS THE LOVE	BILL ANDERSON (MCA 40893)	28	4
20	IT ONLY HURTS FOR A LITTLE WHILE	SONNY JAMES (Columbia 3-10703)	19	10
21	I'LL BE TRUE TO YOU	MARGO SMITH (Warner Bros. WBS 8555)	27	4
22	NOW YOU SEE 'EM, NOW YOU DON'T	OAK RIDGE BOYS (ABC AB-12350)	26	6
23	FOUR LITTLE LETTERS	ROY HEAD (ABC AB-12346)	29	8
24	BORN TO BE WITH YOU	STELLA PARTON (Elektra E-45468)	23	9
25	I'VE GOT TO GO	SANDY POSEY (Warner Bros. WBS 8540)	24	11
26	SLOW AND EASY	BILLIE JO SPEARS (United Artists UA-X1190-Y)	31	6
27	UNCHAINED MELODY/SOFTLY, AS I LEAVE YOU	RANDY BARLOW (Republic REP-017)	34	8
28	DIRTY WORK	ELVIS PRESLEY (RCA PB-11212)	8	9
29	I BELIEVE IN YOU	STERLING WHIPPLE (Warner Bros. WBS 8552)	35	6
30	I LIKE LADIES IN LONG BLACK DRESSES	MEL TILLIS (MCA-40900)	45	2
31	HERE COMES THE REASON I LIVE	BOBBY BORCHERS (Playboy ZS8-5827)	30	7
		RONNIE McDOWELL (Scorpion/GRT 160)	68	4

#	Title	Artist	Weeks On 5/13	Chart
32	LET ME BE YOUR BABY	CHARLY McCLAIN (Epic 8-50525)	37	11
33	SHADY REST	MEL STREET (Polydor PD 14468)	39	5
34	IT'S A HEARTACHE	BONNIE TYLER (RCA PB-11249)	40	5
35	I'D LIKE TO SEE JESUS (ON THE MIDNIGHT SPECIAL)	TAMMY WYNETTE (Epic 8-50538)	41	3
36	I'LL NEVER BE FREE	JIM ED BROWN/HELEN CORNELIUS (RCA PB-11220)	11	12
37	WHISKEY TRIP	GARY STEWART (RCA PB-11224)	13	11
38	ONLY YOU	FREDDIE HART (Capitol P-4561)	44	5
39	BABY I'M YOURS	DEBBY BOONE (Warner/Curb WBS 8554)	46	5
40	EVERY TIME TWO FOOLS COLLIDE	KENNY ROGERS AND DOTTIE WEST (United Artists UA-XW1137)	25	14
41	COUNTRY LOVIN'	EDDY ARNOLD (RCA PB-12257)	53	3
42	RISING ABOVE IT ALL	LYNN ANDERSON (Columbia 3-10721)	48	5
43	MAYBE BABY	SUSIE ALLANSON (Warner/Curb WBS-8534)	33	12
44	COME ON IN	JERRY LEE LEWIS (Mercury 55021)	22	11
45	RUNAWAY	NARVEL FELTS (ABC AB-12338)	32	10
46	IT JUST WON'T FEEL LIKE CHEATING (WITH YOU)	SAMMI SMITH (Elektra E-45476)	49	5
47	TOO MANY NIGHTS ALONE	BOBBY BARE (Columbia 3-10690)	58	5
48	THINK I'LL GO SOMEWHERE (AND CRY MYSELF TO SLEEP)	BILLY "CRASH" CRADDOCK (ABC AB-12357)	59	3
49	WEEK-END FRIEND	CON HUNLEY (Warner Bros. WBS-8572)	57	2
50	THE LOSER	KENNY DALE (ABC AB-12357)	61	4
51	SLIPPIN' AWAY	BELLAMY BROS. (Warner/Curb WBS 8558)	60	3
52	TONIGHT	BARBARA MANDRELL (ABC AB-12362)	—	1
53	NEVER MY LOVE	VERN GOSDIN (Elektra E 45483)	69	3
54	I WILL NEVER MARRY	LINDA RONSTADT (Asylum E-45479)	77	2
55	YOU NEEDED ME	ANNE MURRAY (Capitol P-4574)	71	3
56	EASY	JOHN WESLEY RYLES (ABC AB-12348)	56	5
57	I CAN'T GET UP BY MYSELF	BRENDA KAYE PERRY (MRC MR-1013)	72	3
58	(THE TRUTH IS) WE'RE LIVIN' A LIE	R.C. BANNON (Columbia 3-10714)	73	3
59	DON'T MAKE NO PROMISES (YOU CAN'T KEEP)	DON KING (Con Brio CBK 133)	68	4
60	IF THERE'S ONE ANGEL MISSING (SHE'S HERE IN MY ARMS TONIGHT)	BILLY PARKER (SCR SC-157)	64	5
61	THREE SHEETS IN THE WIND	JACKY WARD & REBA McENTIRE (Mercury 55026)	76	2
62	YOU'LL BE BACK (EVERY NIGHT IN MY DREAMS)	JOHNNY RUSSELL (Polydor PD 14475)	80	2
63	THAT'S WHAT MAKES THE JUKE BOX PLAY	MOE BANDY (Columbia 3-10735)	—	1
64	MAYBE I SHOULD'VE BEEN LISTENIN'	RAYBURN ANTHONY (Polydor PD 14457)	36	10
65	HEARTS ON FIRE	EDDIE RABBITT (Elektra E-45461)	43	14

With Brooks & Dunn in a promotional photo and on stage.

Fashion and Friendship

Sandi Spika, 1995.

Sandi Spika became much more than Reba's go-to stylist. For more than thirteen years, Spika traveled with Reba as her personal fashion designer, hair stylist, and close friend. Spika accompanied Reba on tour, helping her prepare for concerts and navigate tricky costume changes. She worked with Reba on photo shoots, movie sets, award shows, and countless TV appearances.

"She liked for me to work with her all the time, to design for her and help her with all of her clothing," Spika said. "We were more like sisters. We were, and are, such good friends and a fierce team."

In 1987, Spika was a recent graduate of the University of New Mexico and working as a fashion buyer when she handed Reba a portfolio of clothing design sketches following an Albuquerque concert. Reba liked what she saw in the portfolio and comissioned Spika to create a stage gown. "I made it and sent it to her, without having a fitting," Spika recalled. "I did not know for a long time if Reba actually wore it."

Months later, Spika saw a photo of the dress she created, in a tour book. Reba wore the new black suede gold-fringed outfit at her Carnegie Hall debut and other shows in 1987. After filling more orders for Reba, Spika came to Nashville for a fitting at the singer's invitation. When the two met, Reba made a proposal. "Would you consider coming to work for me?" she asked Spika, who accepted, asking if she could try it for six months.

Sandi with Reba, dressed as Lucille Ball for a skit, "I Love Flucy," from a 1995 CBS Thanksgiving TV special.

At the McEntire ranch in Oklahoma. Standing: Narvel Blackstock. Middle, from left: Reba's niece Calamity McEntire; Reba's mother, Jacqueline McEntire; Reba; niece Autumn McEntire. Front, from left: Sandi Spika; Reba's sister Susie McEntire-Eaton.

Right: Sandi with Kenny Rogers and Reba, on the movie set for *The Gambler Returns*, 1991.

Sandi with Linda Davis and Reba on the set of the video for "Does He Love You," 1993.

Right: Sandi and Reba preparing for a stage entrance during a concert, 1998.

A sampling of stage gowns and fashion sketches by designer Sandi Spika, 1987–1993.
Dress photos by Bob Delevante.

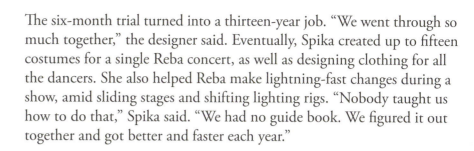

The six-month trial turned into a thirteen-year job. "We went through so much together," the designer said. Eventually, Spika created up to fifteen costumes for a single Reba concert, as well as designing clothing for all the dancers. She also helped Reba make lightning-fast changes during a show, amid sliding stages and shifting lighting rigs. "Nobody taught us how to do that," Spika said. "We had no guide book. We figured it out together and got better and faster each year."

In addition to designing for Reba, Spika created costume designs for other artists, including Linda Davis, Faith Hill, Martina McBride, Kenny Rogers, Trisha Yearwood, and others.

Gowns and sketches by Sandi Spika for Reba, 1994 and 1995. *Dress photo by Bob Delevante.*

Above: Reba and Sandi during the filming of the TV movie *Buffalo Girls*, 1995.

Gowns and sketches by designer Sandi Spika for Reba, 1996–2000.
Dress photo by Bob Delevante.

Above: Reba with George Flanigen (left) and Robert Deaton (second from right) of Deaton Flanigen Productions during a birthday celebration for Sandi.

Left: Reba and Sandi underneath a stage on Reba's co-headlining tour with Brooks & Dunn, 1998.

Left: Sandi touching up Reba's hair on the set of the video for "What If It's You," 1997.

Below: Note to Sandi from Reba, 1998.

Opposite: Reba wearing a Sandi Spika-designed gown on the set of the video for "If I Were a Boy," 2011.

These days, Spika is senior vice president of creative services at Big Machine Label Group, where she works with the Band Perry, Brantley Gilbert, Rascal Flatts, Taylor Swift, Tim McGraw, and others; she is married to the company's founder and president, Scott Borchetta. In November 2008, Reba signed with Valory Music, part of BMLG, reuniting the singer with Spika and her husband, who had been a promotion executive at MCA during the height of Reba's sales success in the 1990s. Spika designed the elegant gown Reba wore in the video for the 2011 single "If I Were a Boy."

Spika draws on her Reba experiences when she works with new artists on the Big Machine roster. She helped introduce artists such as Taylor Swift to the art of quick changes. "Each music artist is unique," Spika said, "and I enjoy helping them with their image and performance visions."

Life on Top

Reba helped introduce a high-tech production style to country music concerts in the late 1980s, and she stayed on the cutting edge through the 1990s. Each tour seemed more spectacular than the previous one.

"My concerts are very theatrical," she said in a 1994 interview. "I've always wanted it to be a stage production, like a Broadway show. We don't just sing song after song; we tie them together with a prop or a costume or some dialog. We link everything together into one continuous show."

She also tackled other creative fields. Besides her ongoing acting roles in movies and network specials, Reba starred in a high-profile TV commercial for Frito-Lay in 1994, complete with intricate choreography. She also published her autobiography, *Reba: My Story*, the same year.

As hard as she had worked through the 1980s and 1990s, and as many new ventures as she had undertaken, the ambitious entertainer from small-town Oklahoma was far from slowing down. She still had several new challenges and surprises in store.

Right: Reba's sponsorship ties with Frito-Lay included having her image featured on snack bags.

Top right: The autobiography *Reba: My Story*, co-written with Tom Carter, 1992.

With her 1998 Minnie Pearl Award, presented for outstanding community service, at the TNN/*Music City News* Awards.

Sitting in empty arena, mid-1990s.

Clockwise from above: Holding her awards for Entertainer of the Year and Female Vocalist of the Year at the 1994 ACM Awards; Reba on stage in 1993; a close-up of her blue-beaded stage jacket, designed by Sandi Spika; her 1994 ACM Entertainer of the Year trophy.
Jacket and trophy photos by Bob Delevante.

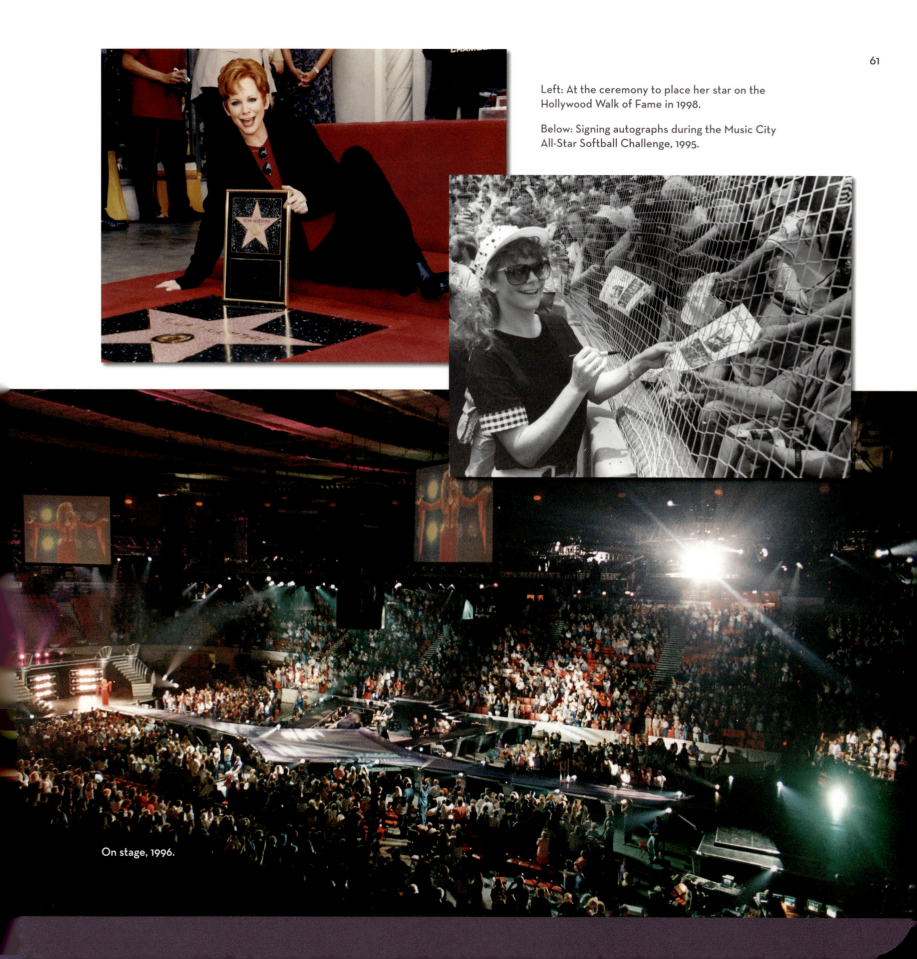

Left: At the ceremony to place her star on the Hollywood Walk of Fame in 1998.

Below: Signing autographs during the Music City All-Star Softball Challenge, 1995.

On stage, 1996.

With co-star Kenny Rogers in the TV movie *The Gambler Returns: The Luck of the Draw*, 1991

Acting

Drama Queen

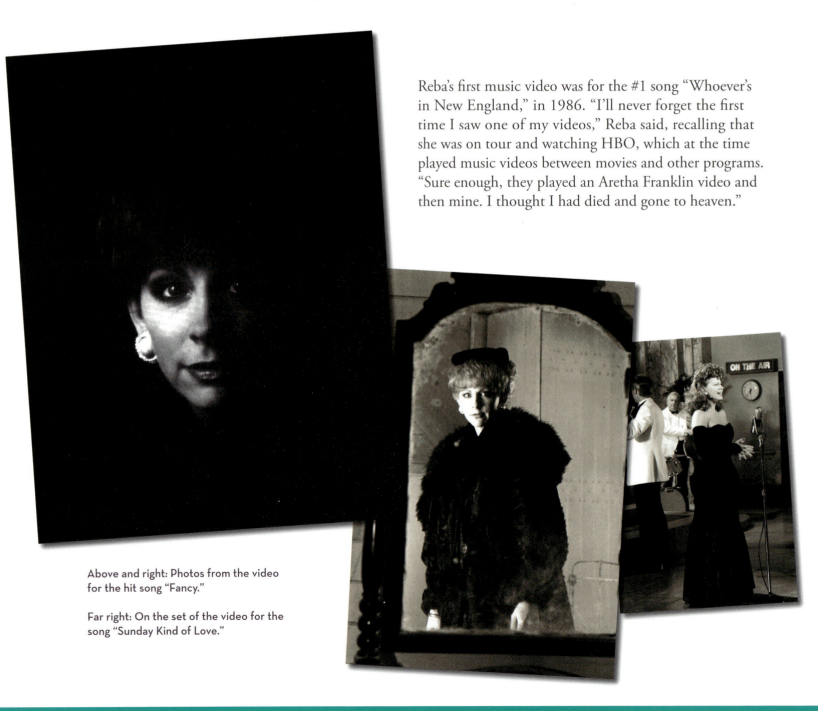

Reba's first music video was for the #1 song "Whoever's in New England," in 1986. "I'll never forget the first time I saw one of my videos," Reba said, recalling that she was on tour and watching HBO, which at the time played music videos between movies and other programs. "Sure enough, they played an Aretha Franklin video and then mine. I thought I had died and gone to heaven."

Above and right: Photos from the video for the hit song "Fancy."

Far right: On the set of the video for the song "Sunday Kind of Love."

Reba's fans all have their favorite videos: the dramatic return home in "Fancy"; the range of emotions displayed in "Is There Life Out There"; the arch drama and glamour of "Does He Love You"; and the humor and outrageous stage costumes, hairdos, and choreography of "Why Haven't I Heard from You?"

Reba's work in music videos prepared her for greater acting challenges and proved that her multiple talents would come across well on film, TV, and stage.

With director Jon Small on the set of the music video "It's Your Call," 1993.

Top left: "Why Haven't I Heard From You," music video, 1994.

Left: Reba sitting for her transformation into an elderly woman, in the music video for the song "The Night the Lights Went Out in Georgia," 1992.

Expanding Her Roles

Reba's professional acting career started with a small step but soon leapt forward. In the comic horror film *Tremors*, she played a small but noteworthy role outside of her own personality or experience. Shortly afterward, Kenny Rogers invited her to co-star in *The Gambler Returns: The Luck of the Draw*, the 1991 installment of his TV movie franchise.

Reba returned to the big screen in the big-budget 1994 feature *North*, directed by Rob Reiner. The film received mixed reviews, but Reba garnered positive reaction for her portrayal of the colorful wife of a wealthy Texas oil man played by Dan Ackroyd.

Previous page: With actor Michael Gross, as survivalist couple Heather and Burt Gummer, in *Tremors*.

Top left: Behind a Gatling gun in *The Gambler Returns*.

Left: Poster for *The Gambler Returns: The Luck of the Draw*, 1991.

As Ma Tex in the film *North*, 1994.

From there, she continued to balance film and TV roles. She made cameo appearances in *Little Rascals* and *One Night at McCool's*. In TV films, she co-starred in the western film *Buffalo Girls*, playing legendary cowgirl Annie Oakley, took lead roles in *The Man from Left Field* with Burt Reynolds; *Is There Life Out There?* with Keith Carradine; *Forever Love* with Bess Armstrong and Tim Matheson; and *Secret of Giving* with Thomas Ian Griffith and Ronny Cox.

Reba may have missed her biggest film role when she had to cancel plans to play Molly Brown in *The Titanic*. Director James Cameron initially cast Reba in the role, but when production times changed, Reba had to back out to honor previous concert commitments. Actress Kathy Bates replaced her. Still, Reba had major roles to come.

Top: Reba as Annie Oakley, Peter Coyote as Buffalo Bill Cody, and Anjelica Huston as Calamity Jane, from the TV movie *Buffalo Girls*, 1995.

Above: With actors Bug Hall (left), as Alfalfa, and Travis Tedford, as Spanky, in the film *The Little Rascals*, 1994.

Reba as single mother Rose Cameron, Devon Alan as son Toby Cameron, and Thomas Ian Griffith as mysterious drifter Harry Withers, from the TV movie *Secret of Giving*, 1999.

On Broadway

Reba accepted an invitation to portray celebrated western sharpshooter Annie Oakley in a Broadway revival of the Irving Berlin musical *Annie Get Your Gun*. She first appeared on January 26, 2001, becoming the fourth actor to play Annie in its revival, following the 1999 opening with actress Bernadette Peters in the lead role.

In the *New York Times*, critic Ben Brantley said Reba glided into the role "like a seabird landing on water," adding that the country star "managed to put a highly personal, proprietary stamp on a role that the ghost of Ethel Merman has always dominated, creating the most disarmingly unaffected Annie in years." The reaction throughout her exhausting five-month run was similarly superlative. "When she stepped into *Annie Get Your Gun* on Broadway," wrote critic Kenneth Jones in *Playbill*, "her name rocketed to the pantheon of great ladies of the American musical theatre."

Above: *Playbill* magazine, May 2001.

Left: As Annie Oakley in *Annie Get Your Gun*, 2001.

Promotional photo for *Annie Get Your Gun*.

On stage at the Marquis Theatre, on Broadway in New York.

Right: Western jacket worn in promotional photos for *Annie Get Your Gun*.

Above right: With actor Larry Storch, as Sitting Bull.

With husband Narvel Blackstock and son Shelby, in Reba's dressing room.

Left: Western gown from *Annie Get Your Gun*
Photo by Bob Delevante.

Reba was not eligible for a Tony Award for her performance in *Annie Get Your Gun* because she did not originate the role. But she did win a prestigious 2001 Drama Desk Special Award, which honors individuals and organizations that make an exceptional contribution to the theater.

Reba Triumphs on TV

Reba's success on the Broadway stage ushered in another challenge: could she carry a TV sitcom on her own? The answer was a resounding yes, as she proved with her extended run as the star of the half-hour series *Reba* on the WB network.

Playing Reba Hart, a quick-witted single mother, Reba headed a Houston household while dealing with the shenanigans of a shallow ex-husband, his ditzy, young second wife, and three rambunctious children—the oldest of whom became pregnant as a high-school senior in an early episode.

Reba set a record for Friday viewership on the WB and often ranked as the most-watched cable program in its timeslot. Ratings remained strong after five years, when WB and UPN merged to form the CW network. Although *Reba* ranked as the top-rated sitcom on CW, the show was canceled when the network decided to focus on teen dramas, reality shows, and Friday-night wrestling programs.

Above: The cast of *Reba*. Back row, from left: Steve Howey, Christopher Rich, and Melissa Peterman. Front row: Joanna Garcia Swisher, Reba, Mitch Holleman, and Scarlett Pomers.

Promotional image for season six of *Reba*, 2006.

Standing: Steve Howey, Christopher Rich, Melissa Peterman.
Seated, middle: Joanna Garcia Swisher, Scarlett Pomers.
Seated, front: Reba, Mitch Holleman.

Scenes from episodes of *Reba*.

Singing "Honey Bun" in the second act of *South Pacific* at Carnegie Hall.

South Pacific

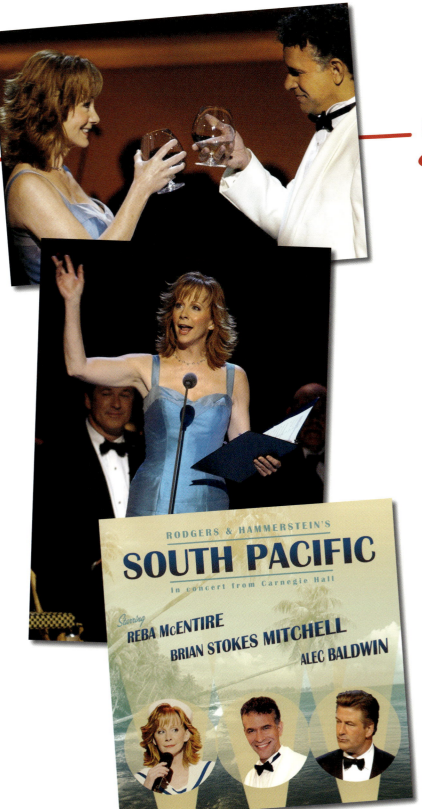

Predictably, considering her reviews for *Annie Get Your Gun*, Reba received several offers to perform in other musicals, but the production schedule of her TV show made such a commitment impossible. However, the singer did make time in 2006 for a one-off performance of *South Pacific*, a Richard Rodgers and Oscar Hammerstein II musical that won a Pulitzer Prize and ten Tony Awards in its original 1950 production. Co-starring Alec Baldwin and Brian Stokes Mitchell, the TV show was taped live and broadcast the following year as part of PBS's *Great Performances* series. The album *South Pacific: In Concert from Carnegie Hall* became a solid seller.

Reba starred as Nellie Forbush, an army nurse from Arkansas stationed on a South Pacific island in World War II. She falls for an older French expatriate plantation owner with mixed-race children. The production included such classic songs as "Some Enchanted Evening," "I'm in Love with a Wonderful Guy," and "I'm Gonna Wash That Man Right Outta My Hair," all showcase numbers for Reba.

Top: Brian Stokes Mitchell, as Emile de Becque, toasting with Reba's Nelly Forbush.

Middle: Reba performs while Alec Baldwin, as the charming U.S. Marine Luther Billis, looks on.

Left: The cover of the album *South Pacific: In Concert from Carnegie Hall*.

A Return to Comedy

Contemporary country star Blake Shelton on set with (from left) Lily Tomlin, Juliette Angelo, and Reba in the *Malibu Country* episode "Oh Brother."

Reba McEntire graduated to network television with ABC's *Malibu Country*, her return to a lead role in a half-hour situation comedy. She starred as Reba MacKenzie, a former country singer who gave up her career for her husband, a country star played by Jeffrey Nording. When Reba discovers that her husband has cheated on her, the two divorce. In the settlement Reba gets the couple's home in Malibu, California, and she moves into the house with her mother (played by Lily Tomlin) and teenage children: son Cash (Justin Prentice) and daughter June (Juliette Angelo).

Outfit worn by Reba in episode three, "Based on a True Story."
Photo by Bob Delevante.

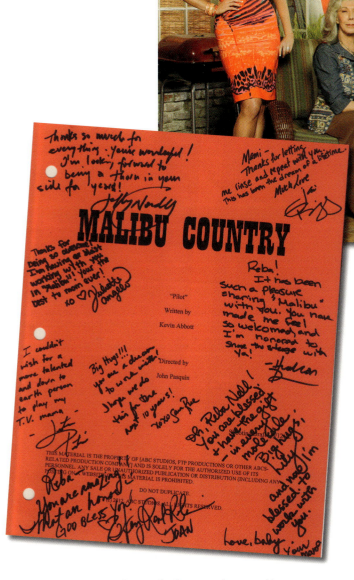

Malibu Country cast, from left: Sara Rue, Lily Tomlin, Reba, Justin Prentice, Juliette Angelo, and Jai Rodriguez.

Script of pilot episode, signed by cast.

Reba's character strives to restart her country music career while raising her spirited teens and enduring her mother's disparaging wisecracks. Guest stars included Blake Shelton, who played Reba's troublemaking brother Blake MacKenzie, and Laura Bell Bundy as a hot young country star with bad habits, who guides Reba's kids toward inappropriate behavior.

Reba performed the show's theme song, "Goodbye Looks Good on Me." The series premiered on November 12, 2012. ABC decided not to renew the series, and the last of the eighteen episodes aired on March 22, 2013. "I had a wonderful time working on *Malibu Country* with the great Lily Tomlin," Reba said. "We all loved our job and hated to see it come to an end. Everything happens for a reason."

Photo session for album cover of *So Good Together*, 1999.

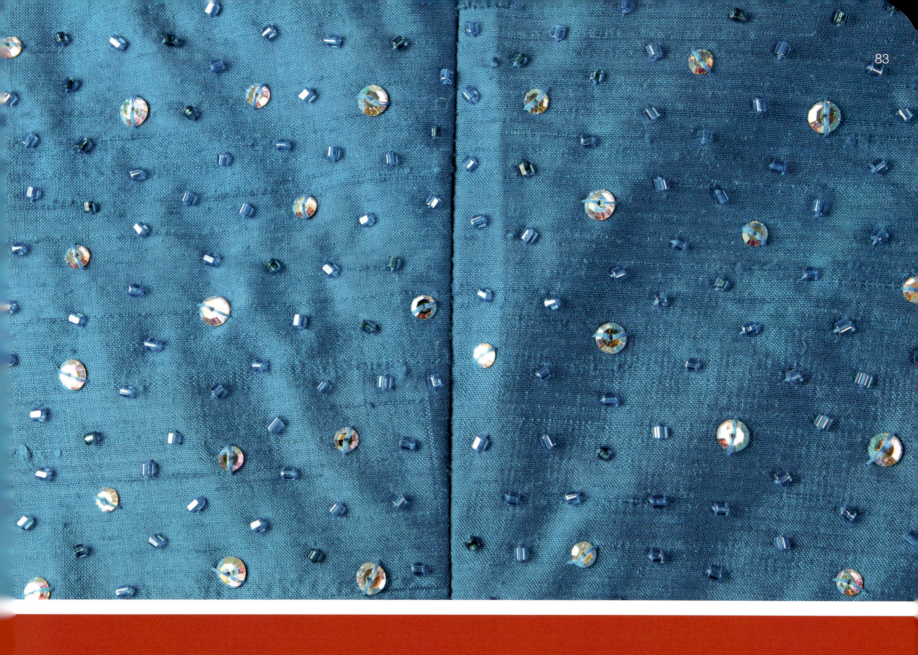

American Icon

A Musical Journal

After a decade of extravagant musical spectacle, Reba decided to tone down her concert performances in 1999. On the *Singer's Diary* tour, she presented an intimate, autobiographical, two-hour show that followed her life from ranch to riches.

The first half of the program featured songs interspersed with personal stories, family photos, and home-video clips. Reba mixed hits and select covers to comment on the details of her story. She sang the national anthem when discussing her discovery at a rodeo championship, and she offered an emotional take on "The Greatest Man I Never Knew," talking about her father's solid but stoic personality. The second half of the show was a more conventional concert, including recent hits.

Reba enjoyed the experience so much that she continued to give fans a more intimate, less flashy show. The production remained state-of-the-art: Reba still changed costumes; she still had dancers and choreography; parts of the stages still moved; and she still liked an element of surprise and theatricality. But the new century brought a measure of understatement markedly different from the flamboyant exhibitions of the 1990s.

The *Singer's Diary* tour, 1999.

In the spotlight.

Still Climbing Mountains

Reba began the new century with her third greatest-hits collection, a mark of her longevity as a star and hit-maker. The album featured two new tracks, including the #3 hit "I'm a Survivor," a song custom-fit for how the singer continued to find ways to stay on top. "I'm a Survivor" also provided the TV Show *Reba* with its theme song.

However, the commitment required to star in her self-titled TV sitcom left little time for creating music in the early 2000s. She ended a hiatus from recording with 2003's *Room to Breathe*, her first album of all-new material in four years. Her return to the radio charts came with the hit "I'm Going to Take That Mountain," another song about striving toward goals.

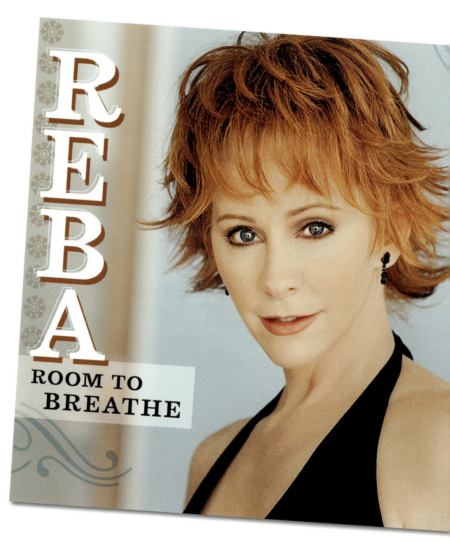

The cover of the album *Room to Breathe*, 2003.

Left: Receiving CMT's Johnny Cash Visionary Award, 2004.

With Carole King (top), Justin Timberlake (middle), and Trisha Yearwood, recording for the *Reba Duets* album in 2007.

Four more years passed before she released *Reba Duets*, an album pairing her with rock, pop, and country stars. The album was her first to debut at #1 on *Billboard*'s all-genre Top 200 album chart.

With Faith Hill, in the studio, 2007.

With Kenny Chesney, 2007.

The Reba Brand

In 2005, Reba accepted an invitation from Dillard's department stores to create a clothing line under the new Reba Lifestyle brand.

"I like to wear what feels good," Reba said at the time of her clothing line's launch. "If I feel good in what I'm wearing, I have more confidence, whether I'm going on stage, to a meeting, or out with my family. I know what works for me, and I want to translate that into what will work for other women, too."

As the singer's relationship with Dillard's and its customers evolved, the Reba brand grew to comprise Reba Luggage, Reba Footwear, and Harmony for the Home, which includes home furnishings and kitchen and bedroom collections.

Right and far right: Leather jacket, with rhinestones and embroidery, from the Reba Lifestyle brand for Dillard's.
Jacket photo by Bob Delevante.

Above: Dillard's promotional ad for Reba Lifestyle brand.

Clockwise, from top right: Reba brand bedding, boots, and shoes.

Promotional image from 2009, when Reba hosted the ACM Awards for the eleventh time.

An Entertaining Host

Reba first hosted the Academy of Country Music Awards in 1986, at a time when she and the annual show were both climbing in popularity and figuring out how they fit into the entertainment world at large. Hosting that event also started Reba's long and cherished relationship with TV legend Dick Clark, whose company produced the ACM Awards.

dick clark

May 20, 2008

I can't believe they had you back after nine previous attempts to successfully host the Academy of Country Music Awards, Reba. Then again, I guess practice makes perfect!

Seriously, you were terrific as usual. I wish I could have been there to personally compliment you on a wonderful performance. Congratulations on another great job!

LOVE—
Dick

Ms. Reba McEntire

Letter to Reba from Dick Clark, who began producing the ACM Awards in 1979.

With Dick Clark in 1986 (above) and 2004 (right).

Hosting the ACM Awards, 2009.

On her fourth wardrobe change at the 2012 ACM Awards.

Promotional image of co-hosts Blake Shelton and Reba McEntire for the 2012 ACM Awards.

Hosting the ACMs in 2012.

In 1999, after some years away, Reba returned as host of the awards night, and she proved so popular and likable that she continued in that role through 2010. For her last two years as host, 2011 and 2012, she shared the stage with Blake Shelton, another Oklahoma country star whom she considered a close friend and whose career her husband and oldest son managed.

In 2013, after taking the starring role in the situation comedy *Malibu Country* on ABC, Reba bowed out of her ACM hosting duties. She remains an Academy favorite: she has won the ACM Top Female Vocalist honor a record seven times, and Entertainer of the Year once.

The Academy also has given her three special awards: She was the first winner of the Home Depot Humanitarian Award, in 2002; she was given an ACM Leading Lady Award in 2003; and she received a special honor in 2005 recognizing her achievement for winning Top Female Vocalist more than any other artist.

Two Close Friends, Two Strong Voices

When Kelly Clarkson rolled toward victory in the first season of the *American Idol* talent competition in 2002, she continually cited Reba as an influence and hero. But she couldn't have known just how entwined their futures would become.

After winning *Idol*, Clarkson backed up her comments by inviting Reba to join her in an *American Idol* TV concert special on Fox that same year. The two performed "Does He Love You," the award-winning hit Reba previously recorded with Linda Davis.

Reba remained a friend and confidant, and in 2007 Clarkson switched her management to Starstruck Entertainment, run by Reba's husband, Narvel Blackstock. Clarkson made those ties even tighter when she became engaged in December 2012 to Brandon Blackstock, Narvel's son and Reba's stepson.

After Reba and Clarkson recorded a 2007 duet of one of Kelly's biggest hits, "Because of You," the two embarked on a national concert tour. Playfully acknowledging that they came from two different genres—country and pop—the friends billed their concerts as the *2 Worlds 2 Voices Tour*.

They shared a band and the stage throughout, performing each other's songs together. The tour began in January 2008 and staged thirty-nine concerts through November of that year. The first fifteen shows were sellouts, and the entire tour proved successful for both artists.

Recording the duet hit "Because of You" with Kelly Clarkson, 2007.

Right: All-access pass from the *2 Worlds 2 Voices Tour*.

With Kelly Clarkson on stage (top), on a video set (above), and in a promotional photo.

Connecting to a Big Machine

Promotional images for Valory Music Company, and the cover of the album *All The Women I Am*, 2010.
Photos by Russ Harrington.

After twenty-five years with MCA Records, Reba left to sign a contract with the hottest new record company in country music. In November 2008, she formed a partnership with Big Machine Label Group, home to Taylor Swift and Rascal Flatts. She announced that she would record for Valory/Starstruck, which combined a BMLG subsidiary with her longtime company.

Reba's band, 2013 (from left): Jeff King, Jimmy Mattingly, Bruce Bouton, Catherine Marx, Reba, Jennifer Wrinkle, Doug Sisemore, Mark Hill, Tommy Harden, and Jim Kimball.

The move reunited Reba with Big Machine founder and president Scott Borchetta and his wife, Sandi Spika Borchetta. Scott had been senior vice president of promotion at MCA in the 1990s; Sandi had been her longtime friend, stylist, and traveling companion and now served as Big Machine's senior vice president.

"I am thrilled to be joining the Valory team," McEntire said when making the announcement. "Scott and I worked together on some of the biggest singles of my career, and I am excited to renew our partnership."

The Borchettas were just as enthusiastic. "If it wasn't for Reba, I would've never met my husband," Sandi said. "It's so great to be working together again."

Reba's first Valory album, 2009's *Keep on Loving You*, yielded two Top Ten hits—the title cut and "Consider Me Gone," her first #1 hit in five years. She scored another #1, "Turn on the Radio," with her 2010 album, *All the Women I Am*.

Big Machine president Scott Borchetta, Reba, Sandi Spika Borchetta, and Narvel Blackstock.

Top: With Taylor Swift and Borchetta.

In concert, 2010.

Top of the Mountain

Reba's induction into the Country Music Hall of Fame on May 22, 2011, capped a growing list of honors recognizing her stature as one of the most enduring and successful artists of her time. Other awards based on career achievement include: ACM Leading Lady Award, 2003; ACM Milestone Award for most Female Vocalist wins, 2005; *Billboard* Woman of the Year, 2007; and ASCAP Golden Note Award, 2008. She also was the first artist celebrated with a *CMT Giants* TV special, a tribute show filled with performances and spoken accolades from singers she influenced.

At her induction into the Hollywood Bowl Hall of Fame, 2012.

Actor Jimmy Smits presenting Reba with the National Artistic Achievement Award in 2010.

Left: ACM Milestone Award, given to Reba in 2005 in recognition of being named Top Female Vocalist a record seven times. Photo by Bob Delevante.

"Reba has spoken directly to new generations of women, inspiring many to change their lives," said Kyle Young, director of the Country Music Hall of Fame and Museum. "She is the most successful female country performer of her generation. She has achieved more than fifty Top Ten singles and more #1 country albums than any other female artist. She is truly country music royalty."

Dolly Parton inducted Reba during the Hall of Fame Medallion Ceremony, saying, "She's had some of the greatest records I've ever heard. I never get tired of hearing her sing. I've never heard anybody who can put more into a song than Reba. Everybody loves her."

Country Music Hall of Fame class of 2011 (from left): Jean Shepard, Bobby Braddock, Reba McEntire.

Right: Reba outside the Country Music Hall of Fame and Museum, the night she was inducted as a Hall of Fame member, 2011.

Top right: Hall of Fame Medallion.

In accepting her award, Reba reflected on her family and how her father helped her keep success in perspective. She once asked her father what meant more, getting a "trophy buckle" as a steer-roping champion or the work, dedication, and experiences it took to get to that honor. "He said, 'Oh, always getting there.'"

Reba paused, looking over a crowd of family, colleagues, and music-industry peers, and added, "Winning awards is fun. But it's the camaraderie and the people you get to hang out with, the getting there. I agree with Daddy 100 percent."

With family at her Hall of Fame Medallion Ceremony. From left: Shawna Blackstock, Gloria Blackstock, Jackie McEntire, Mark Eaton, Susie McEntire-Eaton, Narvel Blackstock, Reba, Alice Foran, Robert Foran, Justin Smith, Garrett Smith, Shelby Blackstock, Brandon Blackstock.

Celebrating her Hall of Fame induction. Standing, from left: Mark Eaton, Autumn Sizemore, Susie McEntire-Eaton, Gloria Blackstock, Narvel Blackstock, Alice Foran, Chassidy Blackstock Standefer, Melissa White, Brandon Blackstock, Calamity McEntire, Shelby Blackstock. Seated, from left: Chism McEntire, Jackie McEntire, Reba.

Left: Dolly Parton inducted Reba into the Country Music Hall of Fame.
Photos by Donn Jones.

ACKNOWLEDGMENTS

This book and the exhibition it complements represent the contributions of many individuals and organizations. First, we are indebted to Reba McEntire, Narvel Blackstock, and Starstruck Entertainment for their cooperation and support, and for access to the treasure trove of artifacts, documents, photographs, and archival footage on which this exhibition and book are built. Special thanks go to Starstruck Entertainment's Creative Media and Marketing Director Justin McIntosh for his contributions to the effort.

In addition, we are grateful for the artifacts loaned to the museum by Sandi Spika Borchetta. Also, we would like to thank Jake Basden and Big Machine Label Group, and Tom Carter, Reba's co-writer on her autobiography, *Reba: My Story*.

Many museum staff members devoted time and talent to the exhibition and the book alike. Space prohibits listing them all, but some deserve mentioning here. Vice President for Museum Services Carolyn Tate led the exhibition's curatorial team, consisting of principal curator Mick Buck; curators Kayla Wiechmann, Tim Davis, Kelli Hix, and Alan Stoker; registrar Elek Horvath; and production manager Lee Rowe. Vice President for Museum Programs Jay Orr oversaw the work of writer and editor Michael McCall. Creative Director Warren Denney, book designer Emily Marlow, and exhibition designer Margaret Pesek brought their skills to bear as well.

We would also like to thank the Academy of Country Music, the Ford Motor Company Fund, SunTrust, GenSpring, and WKRN, Nashville's News 2, as generous supporters of this exhibition. We are also grateful to the Tennessee Arts Commission and the Metro Nashville Arts Commission for providing essential annual operating support for the museum and helping underwrite publications, school programs, and public programs.